Surfing the Rainbow

Visualization and Chakra Balancing for Writers

T0096977

Surfing the Rainbow

Visualization and Chakra Balancing for Writers

Sue Johnson

**COMPASS
BOOKS**

Winchester, UK
Washington, USA

First published by Compass Books, 2013
Compass Books is an imprint of John Hunt Publishing Ltd., Laurel House, Station Approach,
Alresford, Hants, SO24 9JH, UK
office1@jhpbooks.net
www.johnhuntpublishing.com
www.compass-books.net

For distributor details and how to order please visit the 'Ordering' section on our website.

Text copyright: Sue Johnson 2012

ISBN: 978 1 78099 869 5

A CIP catalogue record for this book is available from the British Library.

Design: Stuart Davies

Printed and bound by CPI Group (UK) Ltd, Croydon, CR0 4YY

We operate a distinctive and ethical publishing philosophy in all
areas of our business, from our global network of authors to
production and worldwide distribution.

CONTENTS

CONTENTS

Dedication

This book is dedicated to all my writing students – past, present and future – and for all those writers I will never meet who are travelling the same pathway.

Definitions

Visualization – a technique that involves focusing on positive mental images in order to achieve a particular goal.

Chakra – any of the seven major energy centers in the body (from Sanskrit word meaning' wheel' or' circle') They correspond to the colors of the rainbow with the base chakra (below the tail bone) being red and the crown chakra violet.

Introduction

Why I wrote 'Surfing The Rainbow'

This book is for anyone who loves writing and wants their work to remain memorable in the hearts and minds of their readers.

It is for anyone who has tried and failed to create the novel of their dreams because the words they initially put on the page do not match the wonderful image in their head. It is for those who feel their writing lacks sparkle.

The book is for those who think their imagination disappeared when they grew up. It is the magic key for rediscovering the way to Storyland.

We are all born creative. The imaginary world of a child is a magical place – where anything is possible. As we get older, many of us are pulled away from this world by well-meaning adults. "Be sensible," we are told. "Stop daydreaming."

Gradually the pathways to that wonderful place get overgrown. We don't go there any more. Our world becomes narrower. Ordinary. We tell ourselves we have no imagination.

Deep inside some of us the dream of writing a novel or becoming an artist or musician lives on – a faint spark in the darkness. "I'll write a novel when I retire", I've heard people say. "I'll start when I've got time."

I wrote this book because I want everyone to know that it is never too early or too late to achieve your creative dreams and have a magical life. If you once had a lively imagination, then it's still there somewhere. You just need to work at setting it free – a bit like oiling a rusty tap so that the water can flow again.

Many good writers are held back by negative messages from the past, or they make the mistake of expecting perfection from a first draft and get disillusioned by Chapter Three when it all looks a bit of a mess. It is possible to challenge and overcome these blockages and move on to a more creative future.

'Surfing The Rainbow' is designed to guide writers along the path towards a completed first draft – and enrich their lives with color, texture and magic at the same time. By following the visualizations and exercises in the book – and writing regularly – you will ease yourself gradually towards a completed story.

Be gentle with yourself and allow the first draft to emerge. Allow ideas to adapt and change. This is all part of the creative process. Stay focused on your ultimate goal.

Many new writers don't realize that creating and editing involve two different parts of the brain. It is usually better to create first, put the work aside for a short time and then go back and tidy up what you have written. If you aim for perfection at each stage you may never reach the end of the book.

Every novel is a different journey, however long you have been writing. You find your own pathway with each one. There are as many different writing methods as there are writers on the planet. There is no 'right' way to do things, so enjoy the discoveries you make along the way – about the story, your characters and yourself.

Keep writing and don't give up!

What you will gain from reading 'Surfing the Rainbow'

I once read that if you've lived to the age of twenty-one, you will have enough material inside you for at least three novels! I believe that stories are a mixture of internal and external influences – the ideas and memories you have grown up with plus the environment you are currently in with its day to day occurrences and the idea for a story that is burning a hole in your brain and will not go away.

Think of every experience you have had in your life – childhood games, school, work, holidays, hobbies, dreams, nightmares - as being potential raw material for stories. Think of your mind as being like a giant compost bin full of an endless supply of ideas that can be transformed into something new.

Use the colors of the rainbow to search for memories that you could use in a novel – for example the green glass bowl on your mother's dressing table could become the one in the story that the main character threw at her husband on the day she discovered he was having an affair with his secretary. A terrified child observing this action might mourn the loss of something she liked looking at, imagining that it once belonged to a mermaid under the sea – before realizing that her life was about to change for ever. Later in the story, when she sees a similar bowl in an antique shop, she gets a flashback to that earlier time in her life.

If you follow the exercises in 'Surfing The Rainbow' and use them regularly, then you will strengthen the pathways in your brain that lead to creative ideas.

'Surfing The Rainbow' encourages you to build writing into your everyday life – a bit like cleaning your teeth. Students who have experimented with these exercises have reported greater happiness in their lives and an appreciation of the world around them. If you are happier, then the people around you will be too.

The breathing and visualization exercises in 'Surfing The Rainbow' will help you in all aspects of your life. For instance, breathing and relaxation techniques can help if you are facing an appointment at the dentist or a job interview. There is scientific evidence to suggest that they can help with problems like blood pressure and anxiety.

Practicing visualization regularly helps to bring creative ideas into focus and show the pathway towards achieving your creative ambitions. Remember that every building on this planet began as an idea in someone's head before it became a reality.

Visualize the cover of your published book – and the steps you need to take towards making this happen. Imagine you are holding the book in your hands. Trace the title on the cover with your finger. What does it feel like? What color is it? Is there a particular image that you could carry with you – either as a picture in a pocket or handbag or re-created as a pendant? Create a series of small steps that you can begin to take towards this. (Daydreaming on its own doesn't work – visualization plus focused action does!)

Before my novel 'Fable's Fortune' was published, whenever I went into a library or bookshop I used to create a physical space for it on the shelves and imagine what it would be like to see it there and be able to pick it up.

The great thing is that visualization is something that can be done anywhere – on a bus or train, in a queue at the supermarket or bank or during a boring meeting.

If you want to give new focus to your writing and your creative life, then by using the exercises in this book – and spending three days on each color – you will be helping to achieve this.

Please note that you don't have to devote hours of time to this. You can achieve a great deal with a short visualization and a fifteen minute writing session every day, especially if you've taken a couple of minutes to plan your next writing session before stopping for the day.

The secret is to write regularly, preferably at the same time of day. Stay playful with your ideas. Remember what you were like when you were a child and captivated by your latest story. Don't judge your writing too harshly, and don't show your work to anyone until you feel ready to do so.

The Seven Rules For Success

Follow these basic rules and you will achieve success with your writing.

1. Identify your writing wishes
2. Clear any blockages from the past
3. Create positive steps towards your goal
4. Make space for your writing in your life
5. Write every day
6. Learn to visualize and build a future vision of yourself
7. Keep going until you succeed

What are your writing wishes?

Imagine it's 'Magic Friday' and you're a published writer.

What does this feel like? Feel free to let your imagination run wild and be wherever and whoever you like.

Are you using a pen name? What is it? Does it make you feel more confident? Does your writing change when you sign your name? What color ink do you use?

Take a few minutes to think about the space you are sitting in. Do you have your own writing room? What is it like? What colors, smells and textures do you notice? What is your desk like? Do you have flowers or a special ornament on it?

How are you dressed? Are you wearing jogging bottoms and a sweatshirt getting ready for a writing session or are you in a red velvet dress going out to do your first book signing? What does it feel like to be successful? Write about this feeling. What color is it? What does it sound like? If it had a taste, what would it be?

Even if it seems a long way off, find something that symbolizes that success and keep it where you can see it. For instance, before my novel 'The Yellow Silk Dress' was accepted for publication, I found an amber necklace in a charity shop that was similar to the one I imagined the heroine of the story wearing and I wore it or kept it in my writing room where I could focus on it for a few minutes every day as I imagined a published version of the book.

Think about the good you will be able to do as a result of your book being published – e.g. help a charity or set up a series of workshops for new writers. If there is a positive benefit from your success then you are more likely to achieve it. Write about the event as if it has already happened. For instance: "I am so pleased that 'The Butterfly Ball' is selling well and making lots of money because I can give a larger monthly donation to the Donkey Sanctuary. For some writers, the idea of their work having a positive benefit to others spurs them on to greater success.

Make a list of your writing wishes every month so that you're taking gradual steps towards your ultimate goal. These could be:

1. Finish a flash fiction story of 250 words.
2. Send it to a competition.
3. Go to a café you've not visited before and see how many ideas you can find.
4. Go to a talk or book signing.
5. Do an outline for a short story.
6. Buy a writing magazine and read it from cover to cover.
7. Experiment with writing a story from a different viewpoint.

8. Write a letter to a magazine
9. Create a story from a childhood memory
10. Visit a gallery and see if a painting inspires a story

Tick each one off as you achieve it and reward yourself for each one. Create a new list. (You may find it helps to do this on the same day each month – or some writers do theirs to coincide with a new moon).

You may find it useful to include non-writing things as well. For instance, if clutter is a problem, then you may find your writing space gains more energy from a spring-clean. If your feet are cold, then you may concentrate on your writing better if you go in search of warm socks. You may gain fresh inspiration from a vibrant picture on the wall above your writing space or a different color on the walls.

What is stopping you?

Many of my students have reported having a critical voice in their heads that has previously stopped them from progressing with their writing. Very often this sounds like a former teacher or a disapproving parent. Some of these messages can be very old – for example a primary school teacher telling someone "You're no good at English," or "You'll never be successful at anything."

Unfortunately, we are more likely to remember negative comments than positive ones. It is said that we need ten positive comments for every negative one in order to maintain equilibrium.

It is important to remember that you have about twenty seconds to deflect comments like this before they begin to do harm. If you know that your sister or a friend might say "Why are you bothering with trying to write anything – you never finish anything" then have a response ready – something like: "I used to be like that when I was younger, but this time it will be different." Imagine yourself with a shelf full of completed projects. Pin the affirmation "I finish what I start" above your workspace. Say it to yourself every morning and before you go to sleep at night.

You may find it helps to imagine what your critic looks like. Draw a picture of them or write a brief description. What is their 'catch-phrase?' Do the same for your creative muse. Imagine your muse as being like a playful child filling loads of pages with lively writing and little sketches and your critic as being like a strict teacher trying to restore order. Imagine the child saying "But I'm having fun…" and the critic saying "You need to be sensible."

Write a dialogue between your muse and your critic. Imagine it being like a scene in a play. Visualize the discussion between the two. Where does this take place? What are their voices like? What do they eat and drink?

Watch as they come to an agreement that pleases both of them. The child is allowed to play with creative ideas and colored pens for as long as they like (imagine the critic doing their knitting or a crossword) and then when the work is complete (and only then) the critic will help to create order and check spelling and punctuation.

My critic sounds very like my old English teacher and her help is invaluable when it comes to editing a manuscript and checking for grammatical errors and typos.

Sometimes people fear that if they tell friends and family they're working on a novel they'll get laughed at and not taken seriously. In this situation, it's probably best to keep what you're doing secret. The funny thing is that if someone has golf lessons nobody expects them to be playing in the Ryder Cup within three months, whereas new writers are often faced with the expectation that they should have written a potential Booker Prize winner within the same time frame.

Create an action plan

Writing a novel can feel like an enormous task. However, like any job, it becomes less scary if you break it down in stages and tackle one bit at a time. Most writers have a quota of words that they aim to achieve every day. If you aim for 1000 words a day, then you will have written enough words for an average length novel within three months.

Put a date in your diary by which time you hope to have a completed first draft.

Treat writing like a serious work commitment – if your boss asked you for a report by a particular date you'd do it, wouldn't you? If you're the sort of person who finds it hard to motivate yourself, then think of a series of treats you could have when you complete each stage. When I was working on the first draft of my first novel I treated myself to a 'little something' every time I completed 5,000 words. (It was amazing how quickly I got them done!)

The important thing is to stay focused on your ultimate goal. Allow yourself to write badly on days when the ideas aren't flowing, you're not feeling good or you have other things on your mind.

Decide on a number of words that you will complete per day or per week. Be realistic about your normal schedule. Don't expect the impossible. It is better to set a lower target and exceed it than to continually fail to meet the figure you have set yourself. Reward yourself for the work you have done – whether you consider what you have written to be good or bad. In order to revise a piece of work, you need to have completed it in the first place! Remember that most first drafts look messy and don't always make sense in places. This is part of the creative process. It doesn't mean that your work is no good. It just means it needs a little more polishing.

Build your identity as a writer. As well as working on your novel, create some shorter pieces of work and send them to magazines. The more pieces of work you have in circulation, the more confident you will feel – and the less concerned about rejection. Enter competitions – many writers get their first breaks from these. I did!

Develop a support network of other writers – either on-line or face to face. You'll find people on the same wave-length as you at book signings, festivals and writing workshops. Look on the internet at writers' blog pages and leave a comment on the ones that interest you.

You could try joining an existing Writers' Circle, but take your time to find one that makes you feel supported and valued and that will encourage you towards publication.

If you don't find one you like, form your own local group or find a 'writing buddy' and meet for coffee or lunch to discuss your writing and read some of your work. Look for someone who will give support and constructive criticism.

Get into good writing habits

Carry a notebook wherever you go and make sure you've got plenty of spare pens! Write whenever you have a few spare minutes. Use the notebook to jot down brief descriptions of people and places and fragments of overheard conversation. If you're in a café look at what people are eating and how they're eating it. Make notes about what color the crockery is and what you can hear and smell.

Artists will usually fill their notebooks with sketches – the salt cellar on the table, a coffee mug, or faces in a crowd. They will usually include notes about colors, tones, weather and the mood they were in when they created the picture.

My own notebooks include a variety of tidbits that help me to create stories and poems – fragments of detail about characters and settings, pressed flowers, scraps of dialogue, postcards and little sketches. They are lively, messy and full of information.

You'll soon discover ideas are like thistledown. You may think you'll remember something until you get home. Trust me – you won't, and a potentially good idea will be lost forever.

When you start work on a novel or longer piece of work, you may find it useful to have a notebook specifically for that story as well as your day to day notebook. Then, if you get a brilliant idea for something that happens in Chapter Two, you'll know where to find it and won't spend valuable time searching through your usual one.

Aim to put something in your notebook every day – a brief description, a few lines of a poem or a good first sentence. Think of it as being like putting money in the bank.

Keep an ideas folder and make notes about possible future projects. If it's an idea that really grabs you then set up a file for it on the computer even if you're working on something else. Buy a box-file and collect articles or pictures that add to the story.

Make space for your writing

Many people tell me that I'm lucky to have the time to write. The truth is that writers don't have any more time in a day than anyone else. They just choose to use that time differently. For instance, I don't own a television because I choose to spend my free time reading, painting and writing.

Begin with small amounts of time and work upwards – a bit like training for a race. You wouldn't go out and run a marathon without any preparation, and the same applies to writing a novel. Start small. All it takes at first is a commitment to write for fifteen minutes a day.

Most people can find this amount of time, even if they have children, full time jobs or neurotic dogs. If you can't find fifteen minutes in one go, then try three slots of five minutes, even if you have to lock yourself in the loo to do it.

If you are on a tight schedule, look at times in the day where you could squeeze a few minutes for yourself. For instance you could:

- get up a few minutes earlier
- go to bed a few minutes later
- write on the train or bus
- write in the car (not while driving!)
- write in the bath
- write while waiting for your children at swimming or

ballet classes
- write while waiting at the dentists

One American writer wrote a non-fiction book during the times that the TV adverts were on. A French minister of state wrote a novel in the half hour that he spent every evening waiting for his wife to finish dressing for dinner.

Once you begin to make space for your writing and start thinking like a writer, you'll discover more opportunities to squeeze in a few more minutes. A lot can be achieved in a short time. If you don't believe me, set the timer for five minutes and see how much paper you can fill.

Write every day

You'll soon notice that certain activities generate the state of mind where ideas flood in. Monotonous household tasks are good for this – ironing, hoovering, dusting and washing up. Driving a regular route can also have the same effect and so can a daily walk if taken alone. The writer D H Lawrence used to volunteer to scrub a friend's kitchen floor if he was stuck. I occasionally resort to sweeping my stair carpet with a dustpan and brush. (The problem usually resolves itself by the time I've gone half way down).

If you're in a situation where it's difficult to put pen to paper, then there are other things you can do to record your ideas. For instance my friend who walks dogs for a living finds it helpful to carry a Dictaphone and record her ideas on it. She types them up as soon as she is able to.

On one occasion when I was without pen or paper I phoned home with an idea for a few lines of dialogue and recorded the information on my answerphone.

Aim to do something towards your writing ambition every day. Even if you only manage three sentences a day, you will still have made a small amount of progress by the end of the week.

Keep pens and paper in every place in your house where you might be able to scribble a few words – in your pocket or handbag, your car, the kitchen, bathroom and beside your bed. Many ideas come when you're just going off to sleep or in those few minutes before you're fully awake.

Keep a list of ideas or subjects to write about so that you're not wasting precious writing time. Write first ideas as quickly as you can. Don't stop to punctuate or edit. Just get the basic story onto the page. As the Australian novelist Kate Grenville says: "It can all be fixed in the morning."

If working on a novel or longer story, you may find it helps to leave the work mid-sentence so that you have something to go on with next time. What I usually do is scribble rough notes for the next bit of the story and then flesh them out when I do the next writing session.

When I'm working on the computer I'll often type these rough notes in bold. Then when I rework them I switch the bold off so that my story lightens up as it progresses towards the second draft.

Stay positive and keep going

You will experience times when it is hard to stay motivated – when you're feeling ill, you get a series or rejections or it seems a long way to the end of the story. This is when your support network helps so much. Also, keep a scrapbook of any successes you've had or encouraging emails. Photocopy any checks you receive in connection with your writing!

I find it helps to read about other writers' journeys. When I was trying to sell my first novel 'Fable's Fortune', I was encouraged by the fact that 'Chocolat' by Joanne Harris was rejected forty times before it was finally published. Looking at how successful that book was – and the fact that it was made into a film - gave me the motivation to keep going with 'Fable's Fortune'.

Make sure that you take any opportunity you can to refill the creative well – a daily walk can help with this, particularly if you take time to notice the moon and stars, the smell of coffee as you pass a little café and the color and texture of flowers in the gardens and hedgerows.

Think about the games you played when you were a child. The horror writer Stephen King uses the places where he played as the inspiration for settings for his novels. Many of these places have now been built on, but they still exist in his imagination.

Get playful. Look at the pictures you can see in clouds. Could you make up a story about them? Play the 'what if' game with furniture and objects that you own. For instance - what if the rug in your sitting room is really a magic carpet that could take you anywhere you wanted to go? How did you discover this? Where have you travelled to?

What if you bought a pair of shoes from a charity shop and they changed your life in some way? What if they took you back in time and you had the chance to marry the man of your dreams? Or what if they took you back to a point in your life when you could change something important? What would you do?

If you're feeling stuck with the project you're working on, try a different type of writing. Create a poem or monologue, write a letter from one of your characters to another. Go out and buy something one of your characters would like and keep it on your writing desk for inspiration. If you usually write romance, experiment with fantasy or crime.

Treat yourself to a really nice coffee mug that makes you feel like a writer.

Don't allow yourself to be put off by negative criticism – the sort of people who dismiss your work without a valid reason.

Learn from any constructive rejections – look on them as part of your apprenticeship as a writer.

Celebrate every success – no matter how small. Each one is a stepping stone on your pathway to success.

Preparing For Visualization

Five minutes

Several well-known writers recommend spending five minutes a day doing absolutely nothing. Many people – particularly women – might feel guilty about doing so, but it can be extremely valuable where generating ideas is concerned. This can work well if done before a writing session because it will take you into a deeper part of your creativity.

This doesn't mean spending five minutes worrying about the tasks you haven't done or the dry cleaning you need to collect on the way home. It means five minutes of being still, doing nothing, clearing your mind of clutter and allowing your subconscious to work properly.

This is good preparation for visualization. You don't need any special clothes or equipment – just a comfortable space to sit where you are not going to be interrupted.

If the 'to do' list keeps intruding then focus on a flower or a color or image from your story.

You may find that fresh ideas come to you by the end of the five minutes. If they do, write them down. Don't worry if you find this difficult at first. It may take a week or two before you start to feel any benefit from it.

Breathing techniques

Practice breathing slowly and deeply. If you reach a stressful point in the day – have a look at what your breath is doing. The chances are you will be breathing only into the top part of your chest and the tension will have brought your shoulders up around your ears!

Slow down.

Breathe in for a slow count of four and breathe out slowly, saying 'calm' or 'peace' to yourself as you do so. (This is something you can do in a bank or supermarket queue – other people are too busy with their own problems to notice what you are doing). Relax your shoulders and notice your heart rate slowing down.

Try to do this a few times during the day – maybe mentally focusing on a flower or a candle flame. You will notice huge benefits from doing so. You will feel calmer, the people around you will be more peaceful and you'll notice a better flow of ideas.

A few minutes' relaxation and slow breathing last thing at night will ensure that you sleep better. If relaxation is a problem for you or you have trouble switching off the images in your head of your 'to do' list, then you may find it helps to repeat the word 'Peace' when you breathe in and 'Calm' when you breathe out.

Alternate Nostril Breathing

I learned this very useful relaxation technique at a yoga class.

Sit in a comfortable position – either cross-legged on the floor if this is comfortable or on a dining chair with your back well-supported and your feet flat on the floor. Close your eyes. Rest your left hand in your lap.

Begin by placing the first and middle fingers of your right hand on your forehead. Close your right nostril with your thumb.

Breathe into the left nostril to a count of four. Close the left nostril with your third finger. Release your thumb. Breathe out through the right nostril to a count of four.

Breathe in through the right nostril to a count of four. Close right nostril with thumb. Breathe out through the left nostril to a count of four.

Repeat this cycle six times breathing slowly and evenly.

Visualization

For this to be most effective, you need a quiet space and no threat of interruption. There is nothing worse than to be in a relaxed state and then have someone barge in and ask: "Are these shirts ironed?" or "What time's tea?"

Early morning can be a good time to practice visualization – before you've had time to store up any distractions.

If it's impossible to get any time on your own at home, or you work full time, then you could park your car somewhere safe and quiet. (Lock the doors!) If all else fails, lock yourself in the loo for a few minutes!

When you get used to doing this on a regular basis, then you will be able to tune into your breathing and meditate or visualize anywhere – even in a crowded railway station or airport.

(The important thing to remember is to make sure that you and your belongings are safe. Don't worry about people thinking you're behaving oddly. In my experience, they're usually too bothered about what they're doing to notice you).

It's better to aim for a short space of time at first as concentration can be difficult. Other thoughts and jobs you need to do crowd in and fight for air time. Again, when you get more used to applying these techniques, you'll be able to go on longer.

Make sure you are warm and comfortable. When you go into a relaxed state, the body can chill very quickly and there is nothing more annoying than being on the point of discovering something new about your story and then being distracted because you are starting to shiver.

You may find it helps to have a special blanket or shawl that signifies visualization time. Have pen and paper handy for when the ideas start flowing. Visualizations are very much more powerful if you prepare for them in advance and then write about the details as fully as you can afterwards. Use the senses as much as you can.

Visualization for success

Every building or structure has been imagined by an architect or designer before it was built. In the same way, we are the architects of our own lives – and our writing success.

I have been told by several well known writers that you make your own luck where being published is concerned – and you do this by being persistent, getting the work done and keeping going until someone says yes.

Dream big dreams by all means – but that alone will not guarantee success. Wishes, dreams and visualizations backed up by structured action will! For instance, if there's a job you really want but it seems out of reach, look at the things you could do to make it achievable e.g. looking at the qualifications you'd need for that job and taking that first step towards getting them.

If your aim is to be a published novelist, then look at the publication history of well-known writers. The chances are that it's taken them several years to be an overnight success – and they probably began by writing short pieces for a local paper or submitting short stories to magazines or competitions.

Visualize yourself as a published writer. Find a picture of 'the outfit' in a magazine and create a 'success collage.' Keep it where you can see it every day.

Write about your visualizations, using as much sensory detail as possible. This will make them much more powerful.

Use positive affirmations – e.g. 'I am creative', 'I am successful,' 'I finish what I start.' Even if you have failed in the past, it is never too late to change. If you find yourself on the receiving end of a comment like "You may never get published," then make sure you counter it with something like "I will keep going until I succeed."

Move away from negative criticism or people who are unsupportive. Move towards people who help and encourage you. You may find that your circle of friends changes as you develop as a writer. Repeat your positive affirmations to yourself at least three times a day. Write them on a piece of paper and keep them in your purse, your underwear drawer and by your writing space.

Create a collage that shows you as a successful writer – with the outfit, the champagne and the fantastic reviews. Display this where you can see it several times a day. (If you think your family may not take this seriously, put it on the inside of your wardrobe door).

Create a small altar by your bed, on a shelf or in the space where you write that symbolizes your writing wishes – this might be a stone with a special message on it – I have one that says 'magic happens' – or an ornament or talisman that encourages you to keep going.

Remember – if you don't take your work seriously and give it space and value in your life then you can't expect anyone else to.

Your writing space

This relates to both your physical writing space and to the creative space writing occupies inside your head.

Regular use of visualization can help with making both spaces more effective.

Just as you need an actual place (or places) to write that doesn't take long to set up, you also need to find a way of reaching that place inside your head where your current story lives as quickly as you can so that you make the most of your writing time.

To start with, you could keep your writing things in a box or special basket or on an old-fashioned tea trolley. Keep everything together so that you don't waste valuable time looking for something.

You may find that it helps to play a short piece of music before you start or light a scented candle as a way of honoring your writing time. Each new project may have a different smell and this may help you to reach your internal space quickly.

I see the space inside my head as a series of pathways leading from a blue wooden gate. If I go in one direction I could be walking on springy grass studded with pink sea thrift on a Cornish cliff-top. A second pathway might take me on a journey through the cobbled streets of Montmartre in Paris. A third pathway leads me to a log cabin in a woodland clearing, which is where I imagine I am when I write. The room smells of patchouli, so that when I light a fragranced candle or sniff a scented sachet, I am immediately transported to that place and the prospect of a new adventure.

Try the following visualization to access your interior writing space:

Writing Space Visualization

(You may find it helps to read this onto a Dictaphone and play it back – or ask a friend with a soothing voice to read it).

Begin by sitting comfortably in a chair. Relax your shoulders. Close your eyes. Let go of any worries or problems for a few minutes and concentrate on your journey. (Some writers like to light a scented candle or incense stick or play soft music in the background).

Have pen and paper beside you before you start.
Focus on your breathing:

Breathe deeply in and out. Allow yourself to relax.
Imagine you are inhaling gleaming white creative energy. As you breathe out, consciously release any tension or anxiety and see it float away as a wispy grey cloud.

Imagine you are leaving your chair, walking out of the door and taking the pathway that stretches ahead of you. Notice what it looks like. How does it feel under your feet? Is it a cobbled street, a wide avenue lined with trees or a pathway through a forest with sunlight slanting through the fresh green leaves?

Follow the path, taking notice of colors, smells, sounds and textures.

You are feeling relaxed as you follow the path. You reach a cross-roads and take the turn to the right. Ahead of you is your writing space. Stand still, breathing slowly and evenly. Take a few moments to look at it, noticing colors and textures.

Move towards the open door and step inside. What smells, sounds and colors do you notice? Remember these as they will be useful to you later.

Sit at the desk and look at the view from the window. What does the chair feel like? Notice the textures of the walls and furniture. What do they remind you of?

Take as long as you like to absorb the images from your special room.

Somewhere in the room is a talisman, to be taken with you when you leave, that will remind you of your special writing space. Take a few moments to find this and carry the image with you in your heart as you get up from your chair and leave the room, closing the door behind you until your next visit.

Follow the path back, noticing the number of steps it takes so that you will remember for your next creative journey. As before, take note of colors, sounds and smells.

Return to your everyday world and sit back comfortably in your chair. Count backwards from 10 to 1 as you start to become aware of your surroundings. Open your eyes. Reach for your pen and write down as much as you can remember about your creative journey, including as much sensory detail as possible, and paying particular attention to the talisman you found.

Make sure that you have a drink and something to eat before you resume your everyday life so that you are properly grounded.

You can return to your writing space as often as you wish to.

Free Write

Start writing before you have fully woken up from your visualization – so that you are in that semi-dreamlike state similar to when you wake after sleep.

Pick up your pen and start writing as quickly as you can. Record every image you can remember – the color of the sky, the scent of a rose, the velvet texture of the chair you were sitting on and the sound of birdsong and carriage wheels. Don't worry about things being in the right order or whether or not they make sense. Just for now, don't worry about spelling or grammar.

Focus on the journey you have just been on. Write about the dusty street lined with wooden planks in the Wild West town and the swing doors of the saloon where a woman in red is dancing… Write about the smell of cassoulet drifting through the open door of a Parisian café and the mournful sound of a violin on the frosty night air…Write about the blue enamel butterfly brooch that the heroine wears that was given to her by the man who broke her heart…

Write as quickly as you can so that you get past that censor in your brain that tells you "That's rubbish! What good is that going to be?" The tiniest detail that you jot down could form the beginning of a scene.

Underline anything interesting. What else can you remember? Keep your visualizations in a special book, folder or envelope.

You will find these useful as a means of developing your 'writing muscle' as well as your story. Start browsing in charity shops for old photographs or pictures that remind you of characters and settings.

Free-writing can be a useful technique if you have a difficult scene to write. Just splurge everything down and then unravel what you want to say from the raw material you have created.

What are the chakras?

Chakra is the Sanskrit word for wheel or circle. The earliest recorded mention of the word is in the Hindu holy books called The Vedas – some of which date back to 3000 BC. It relates to the seven main energy centers in the body that are linked to particular organs or hormone regulators.

Each is associated with a color of the rainbow, a musical note, element and day of the week – creating a rainbow of color and sound inside all of us.

If your chakra "wheels" are spinning freely you will feel healthier, more creative and more able to focus on your work. For this reason, it is important to look after yourself – take regular exercise, eat sensibly and drink plenty of water.

If the chakras are blocked you are likely to feel sluggish or uninspired – and in some cases, ill. If you're feeling seriously ill you must seek medical attention but for those general 'off color days' the exercises in this book, linked with the use of crystals and aromatherapy, may help.

By being aware of the chakras and working through the suggested exercises, you will improve your chances of writing a successful novel as well as having fun and developing a more relaxed attitude to life.

Each section on the chakras relates to a different color of the rainbow and contains a visualization, writing exercises, brief details about crystals and aromatherapy oils and a recipe.

Red Chakra   Take time to prepare well before you start. Clear any blockages that are likely to hold you back.

Orange Chakra   Create a rough outline of the story. Make sure there is enough conflict to sustain the reader's interest.

Yellow Chakra   Create strong and believable characters

Green Chakra   Develop your settings so they are believable too.

Blue Chakra   Make sure your dialogue is convincing.

Indigo Chakra   Use the senses so that the reader has a full picture.

Violet Chakra   Finish what you have started and polish your work so the story flows smoothly.

How to use this information

It is said to take 21 days to create or change a habit. If you are serious about becoming a writer, then this may be what you need to take the first steps towards your new life.

You don't need to commit hours of time. Fifteen minutes a day is good to start with. The important thing is to do this regularly and preferably at the same time of day to begin with.

Think about spending three days on each color to give your writing idea the best chance. If possible, build in a short time for visualization every day before you start writing. Experiment with recipes and scents.

(You can repeat this process as many times as you like to ensure that you and your writing are balanced and full of color and texture).

Red

The Root Chakra

This is situated just below the tail bone and is our grounding point and connection with the earth.

This chakra governs the legs, feet and skeleton, teeth and large intestine. An imbalance here can lead to digestive problems like Irritable Bowel Syndrome or an inability to relax.

The day of the week associated with this chakra is Saturday.

The musical note is C.

Introduce the color red into your workspace by adding a cushion or shawl or piece of stained glass or any of the following crystals:

bloodstone

garnet

red jasper

smoky quartz

ruby

Burn any of the following incense sticks or fragrant oils or use them in your bath:

cypress

mimosa

patchouli

tea tree

Grow a pot of basil on your windowsill or desk. Use the leaves to flavor your cooking. Try the following recipe:

Tomato and Basil Soup

2 onions
clove of garlic
olive oil
2 lbs tomatoes, peeled, deseeded and chopped
2 tbsp tomato puree
chicken or vegetable stock
handful of chopped basil leaves

Sauté the onion in the olive oil until softened. Add the chopped garlic. Add tomatoes and puree and cook for 10 minutes. Add enough stock to cover by a couple of centimeters. Simmer for 15 minutes. Add the basil and liquidize. Season before serving.

Writing Exercises

Use the following as warm up exercises. Set the kitchen timer for three minutes and see how much paper you can fill in the time. Write as quickly as you can. Don't stop.

Writing Exercise 1

Set your kitchen timer. Begin with 'red is...' and keep writing for five minutes. Write as quickly as you can. Don't stop, cross out or censor what you write. If you can't think what to write just start again with 'red is…' until an idea comes to you.

Scribble down everything you can think of about the color red. Stop when the buzzer goes.

Look back at what you have written and underline any bits that interest you.

Is there anything that could become a 'memory' for one of your characters?

Writing Exercise 2

Write about a red dress. Who is wearing it? Where did they buy it? Was it their choice or someone else's? What happened when they put it on? Set the kitchen timer and write down as much information as you can in five minutes. Don't censor what you write – just see what comes out.

At the end of the time, go through what you've written and underline any bits you particularly like. Create a poem, piece of flash fiction or a story from this.

Writing Exercise 3

What was your favorite color when you were a child? Did this change as you got older? Why? What was your least favorite color?

Set the kitchen timer and write about this for five minutes. Could this form part of the background to one of your characters?

Visualization

You may find it helps to read this onto a Dictaphone – or ask someone with a soothing voice to do so.

Have pen and paper beside you for when you've finished.

Sit comfortably in a chair. If possible, take off your shoes. Relax your shoulders. Close your eyes. Breathe deeply in and out. Allow each breath to take you deeper into your creative space as you imagine you are walking slowly along a pathway leading to a wood.

Look carefully at the trees as you reach the wood, noticing colors, sounds and smells. What sort of trees are they? Notice how the trunks rise out of the earth. What colors would you use if you were painting a picture? What texture is the bark? What color are the leaves?

In a small clearing, you notice an oak tree with gnarled roots. There's a space between the roots that looks like a tiny doorway. As you gaze at it, feel yourself growing smaller until you are standing in front of it.

You feel totally safe as you walk towards the doorway. It opens and you walk into the space beyond and find yourself surrounded with soft golden light.

You see a flight of steps curving downwards with a handrail. They are well-lit and you move towards them counting backwards from 30 to zero as you make your way down to the world below.

When you reach the room at the bottom of the staircase, find yourself somewhere comfortable to sit. Visualize the flowing red energy the tree draws from the earth. Think about the space you are in. What can you hear? What smells and colors do you notice?

Somewhere in the room is a message or talisman to encourage you with your new project. Look carefully at this so that you remember every detail.

Say thank you and prepare to return home. Make your way back up the steps counting from zero to 30. Go through the door and close it behind you. As you walk away from the tree, feel yourself return to your usual size.

Follow the woodland path until you reach the place you started from and settle back comfortably in your own chair.

Begin to wake up. Stretch, yawn, wriggle your fingers and toes. Open your eyes. As soon as you feel able, record your journey in as much detail as you can.

The Work

Clear Your Blockages And Get Started

For every 100 novels that are begun, only one is completed. The main reason for this is that the writers did not prepare properly before they started. You wouldn't run a marathon without doing some training first, or plant seeds in the garden without preparing the ground – but a huge number of people embark on writing a novel without a second thought. The problem is that without adequate preparation or developing the writing habit properly, they are likely to get to chapter three and run out of steam. They start with good intentions, but then they get in a muddle, miss a day and then another – and before long they've lost the thread of what they were doing and the shimmer of excitement that had driven them to put pen to paper in the first place has gone.

In all likelihood, by this stage, the critical voice in their head is having a field day by saying "See – I knew you couldn't do it!" If this is added to a list of previous failed attempts, then it may be that a solid wall that says "can't do" has grown up around them like Sleeping Beauty's forest. They admit defeat and give up, thinking that their dream of writing a novel will never come true.

If this sounds like you – then don't despair. You can achieve your dream.

Firstly you need to define the reasons why you want to achieve this particular wish.

Answer the following three questions:

1. Why do you want to write a novel?

2. What is stopping you from moving forward with it?

3. What are you prepared to give up in order to achieve success?

If your answer to the first question is to make as much money as possible, then you may be better to take a computer course at the local college. Writing a book is not necessarily a quick way of making a lot of money. If your answer is something like "Because I won't be happy until I do", then carry on working through this book.

Your answer to the second question may be something like 'lack of time', 'lack of space' or 'lack of support from friends and family.' I wrote the first draft of my first book against a backdrop of all three of these problems. All I'm asking you to do initially is to commit fifteen minutes a day to working through the exercises in this section – adding in five minutes additional time for visualization if possible.

To start with you don't need an office or loads of space. When Maeve Binchy was working on her first novel, she kept her writing things on a tea trolley under the stairs so that she didn't have to waste valuable time looking for anything. (She got up at five o'clock in the morning and worked for two hours before she left home to go to her day job).

If negative messages from your past are still causing you problems, then these need to be dealt with. It's amazing how much harm negative comments from teachers you haven't seen for twenty years can do! Many older people recall remarks made by critical parents. Whoever is causing the problem – it's time for it to stop! Create a persona for the voice and have a dialogue with it. Your old English teacher might be very useful when it comes to editing what you have written, but you don't want her getting in the way of the creative process.

Create positive affirmations for yourself – write them on pieces of card and put them where you can see them. Keep them in your handbag, your dressing table and your car. I have some beautiful stones with affirmations painted on them. They inspire me whenever I see them.

Positive affirmations could include:

I am creative

I am successful

Magic happens

Success magnet

Just do it!

If you are serious about your writing then you could look at your typical day and see where it might be possible to find a small amount of time to write. You don't have to get up as early as Maeve Binchy but you could get up fifteen minutes earlier or go to bed fifteen minutes later.

If your television is on most of the time – are you actually watching every programme? Is there anything you could miss? If you travel by public transport, could you write on the way to work?

Start looking for small pockets of time and make the best use of them that you can.
Keep a list of subjects to write about in your notebook, so that you don't waste valuable time staring at a blank page.

To Do List

Buy a new folder or box file for your new novel.

Set up a folder on the computer for it.

Buy yourself a beautiful notebook and a block of paper to scribble on.

Buy a special pen for hand-writing and felt tips for creating mind maps.

Buy or borrow any research books you need. (Don't get too bogged down in research or you may never get going on the writing. Do as much as you need to get started - and then write!)

Create a 'success' collage to encourage you when you're feeling a bit low.

Think of a working title for your novel.

Create a sound-track for your story that will signify 'writing time' when you hear it.

Decide on a date by which you'd like to finish your first draft. For instance, if your finished book is approximately 90,000 words – if you wrote 1000 words a day you would have it finished in three months.

Make a list of possible treats to encourage you when you've completed each 5000 words. One writing friend of mine buys small items that take her fancy, wraps them in pretty paper, puts them in a special box and then opens one when she feels she has earned a treat.

Orange

The Sacral Chakra

This chakra is situated just below the navel and is ruled by the element water. It controls the blood, bodily fluids, the respiratory system, reproductive organs, kidneys, circulation and bladder. An imbalance can lead to menstrual or sexual problems or the emotions may be suppressed.

The day of the week associated with this color is Monday.

The musical note is D.

Introduce the color to your workspace by buying orange candles or collect the following crystals:

amber

aquamarine

orange calcite

carnelian

coral

moonstone

Burn the following scented candles or use them in your bath:

clary sage

jasmine

rosewood

ylang ylang

Grow a pot of lemon balm on your desk or windowsill. Use lemon zest or juice to spice up your cooking.

Try the following recipe:

Lemon Balm Loaf Cake

Half a cup of butter
Quarter of a cup of chopped lemon balm leaves
1 cup of sugar
2 large eggs
Quarter of a tsp salt
1 tsp baking soda
Half a cup of milk
One and a half cups of sifted self raising flour
Quarter of a cup of chopped walnuts
Grated rind of one lemon

Glaze

Half a cup of sugar
2 tsp chopped lemon balm leaves
Juice of one lemon
1 tsp lemon zest

Method

Heat the oven to 350F. Grease and flour a loaf pan. Cream the butter with the lemon balm. Add sugar, eggs and milk and then add remaining ingredients. Pour into the loaf tin and bake for 35 – 40 minutes.

Remove from the oven. Combine the ingredients to make the glaze and pour over the hot cake while it is still in the tin. Leave for one hour before removing. Serve when cool – or wrap in foil to ripen overnight.

Writing Exercises

Writing Exercise 1

Write down everything you can think of about the color orange. Keep writing for five minutes. Don't stop, cross out or censor what you write. Follow where your memory or imagination takes you.

Writing Exercise 2

Imagine a crescent moon shining on water. Who is watching it? What is their problem or dilemma? Write about this as fully as you can. How is the situation resolved?

Begin by setting the kitchen timer for five minutes and writing as quickly as you can. Don't cross out or censor what you write.

Does anything you have written surprise you? Could it form part of a scene in your novel?

Writing Exercise 3

Create a story about a pot of orange marmalade. Who made it? Who did he/she give it to? Who did they give it to? Think about creating a 'daisy chain' story where the characters are linked by another character who is involved with all the characters in some way – e.g. a taxi driver or cleaning lady. (Look at Maeve Binchy's work for inspiration).

Visualization

You may find it useful to read this onto a Dictaphone or ask someone with a soothing voice to do so.

Have pen and paper ready so that you can record your observations.

Sit comfortably in a chair. If possible, take off your shoes. Relax your shoulders. Close your eyes. Breathe deeply in and out. Allow each out breath to take you deeper into your creative space.

It's a warm moonlit night and you are walking along a sandy pathway that leads to the seashore. Count the number of steps it takes you to reach the beach, going from 0 – 30. Keep breathing in and out as you go along the pathway, noticing the feel of the dry sand on your bare feet.

Small waves lap gently onto the wide expanse of soft golden sand. The moon is full. There is a silver pathway of moonlight across the calm sea. You can smell seaweed and taste salt on your lips as you sit on the warm sand watching the patterns of light on water.

Take a few moments to absorb these images as you breathe

gently in and out.

Let go of any negative feelings that are holding you back with the story you are working on. Breathe them out like grey clouds and see them float away into the night sky to a place where they can do no harm.

Think of a key scene in your new story. Bring this into focus and imagine this taking place on the moon's gleaming pathway as if it were on a stage. Focus on the color orange and imagine the scene being full of energy.

Remember all the details clearly.

Thank the moon for the inspiration she has given you and remember that you can return here whenever you wish to.

Now it is time to make your way back from the beach, along the pathway and into your own space. Count the steps as you return, going from 30 back to 0.
You are now safely back in your own space. Stretch, yawn, wriggle your fingers and toes. Open your eyes. As soon as you feel able, record your journey in as much detail as possible.

The Work

Visualize your story as fully as you can. If you can see the characters and scenes clearly, so will your reader. Take careful note of sensory detail like colors, sounds, smells and textures.

Spend some time looking in bookshops at the books that are similar to yours. (The bookshops that do coffee are the best ones as it is easier to spend longer browsing!) Look at the 'blurb' on the back of the books. What do they tell you? Why would this encourage you to buy them? Make careful notes about the words used and the length of sentences.

There is no 'right' way to write a novel – and you will soon discover that each book is a different journey. You will soon develop your own method of working. Some writers begin with the last chapter and work backwards until they get to the beginning. Others will start at the beginning and keep going until they reach the end. Several people I know begin with a scene in the middle and draw the beginning and ending from it like molten toffee.

I aim to get the first draft of an idea written from start to finish as quickly as I can (usually in 3 – 4 weeks). The result is messy, has more holes than a string vest and may not make total sense to readers at that stage, but it gives me something to work on and develop. I call it my 'Rolling Stone Method' and, to date, I have completed three novels using this method. I hope it helps you too!

The Rolling Stone Method of Novel Writing

1. Begin by writing a 250 blurb for the back cover of your book, including your working title.

2. Create an outline for the whole story in approximately 2,000 – 3,000 words.

3. Put this away for a week or two.

4. When you go back to it, look at it critically and check that there is enough action (plot) to sustain the reader's interest.

5. Look at the time-scale during which the story takes place. Check that the events in the story happen in the right order. If appropriate, look at what is happening in the wider world that could have an impact on the story.

6. When you feel you've got the events in the right order, go back over the story and add more detail. Aim to increase the word count to 10,000 words and then 20,000 words.

7. Go through the main events and list 20 key scenes.

8. Divide the story into chapters and check there is enough dramatic tension.

9. Develop characters and settings.

10. Keep repeating Step 6 until the story reaches the required length.

Reward yourself at each stage of the process.

Ideas about plot and conflict

The basic elements of a story are:

Situation
Complication
Crisis
Resolution

In a novel, there will be a series of complications as the story moves towards the crisis and eventual resolution. There is usually a 'black moment' when it seems that all is lost before the situation is resolved.

Allow your ideas to change and develop. This is normal! The complete plot will only form during the course of writing the book.

Plot is about change, drama and conflict.

If nothing changes by the end of the story, then there is no point in writing it.

Lack of conflict (which means 'not enough happening') is the main reason for a novel being rejected by an agent or publisher.

Don't be afraid to pile the pressure on your characters. Don't allow problems to be solved to easily. Your aim is to keep the reader turning the pages. Remember to release the tension and then bring it back with a vengeance. Look at how Shakespeare achieves this!

Don't rely too heavily on coincidence. The odd one is fine (that's life) but if you do it too often your story and characters will be unconvincing to the reader.

Many writers are worried about the word 'conflict' thinking that it means the characters being deliberately nasty to each other. It doesn't mean this at all, but there does need to be a problem or series of problems to overcome otherwise there will be nothing to interest and captivate the reader.

There are three levels of conflict:

a) A character's battle with some aspect of himself/herself – for example an addiction to credit card spending, habitual lateness or chronic untidiness that gets in the way of them achieving lasting happiness.

b) A character's battle with another person – or more than one! This could be their mother, a potential lover or a new boss.

c) A character's battle with some aspect of their environment – for example bad weather that prevents a character getting to the airport, a car not starting or getting lost in an unfamiliar place.

Find a large piece of paper and make a list of everything that could possibly happen in the story. Take three different colored pens and circle each idea according to which category of conflict they fit. You will then be able to see if you have a balance of conflicts in the story.

Developing more ideas

Try the following techniques for developing more ideas:

Spider Diagram – put a word that symbolizes part of your story in the middle of a blank sheet of paper. Create a 'mind map' from this. This should help you to generate more ideas.

Conflict Circle – If you're not sure what happens next, try drawing a circle on a piece of paper. Divide the circle into eight segments. Write the problem in the middle – e.g. Sally has just lost her job, what does she do next? Then in each of the segments put a possible course of action. On the outer edge of the circle put a reason why she may not take a particular option – for instance she could ask her father for help but they've never got on and she doesn't want to give him the satisfaction of knowing she's failed.

Each Conflict Circle can be re-used to create a different story.

Free-write – If you're not sure exactly what happens in a scene, or it's a difficult one to write, you may find it helpful to do a 'free write.' Write as quickly as you can. Don't worry about spelling, punctuation or grammar. Just get the basic idea onto the page. When you've written everything you know about that scene, go back over your work and underline any words or phrases that interest or surprise you. You may find these useful for creating poems or flash fiction. This should help to clear your mind and get the scene in the right order.

Clustering – This can work as the next step from a 'free-write'. Take a large sheet of paper and start jotting down the fragments of story you can already see. Draw a bubble round each section. Fill in the gaps between sections with diagrams and pictures. You will find this will help you to see new elements of the story..

Spirals – If your ideas aren't flowing because your thoughts are cluttered, it can help to 'free write' in a spiral on a large sheet of paper.

Yellow

The Solar Plexus Chakra

This chakra is ruled by the element of fire and controls the digestion, liver, spleen, gall bladder, stomach, small intestine and metabolism. An imbalance can lead to a lack of confidence and obsessions.

The day of the week associated with this color is Tuesday.

The musical note is E.

Introduce the color to your workspace by buying yellow beeswax candles or any of the following crystals:

citrine

tiger's eye

topaz

Burn the following oils or incense sticks:

cinnamon

juniper

lemon

pine

rosemary

Have a pot of rosemary on your windowsill.

Experiment with recipes using basil, coriander, ginger, peppermint or tarragon. Try the following recipe when working with this chakra.

Ginger Biscuits

6 oz Self Raising flour
4 oz soft brown sugar
1 level tsp bicarbonate of soda
2 oz butter
1 heaped tsp ground ginger
1 tsp golden syrup
1 egg

Mix all the ingredients together apart from the egg.

Beat the egg and add to the mixture bit by bit to form a stiff consistency.

Divide into 12.

Roll each piece into a ball and place on a lightly greased baking sheet.

Flatten slightly.

Bake for 15 minutes on 180C (Gas 4)

Writing Exercises

Writing Exercise 1

Begin with 'yellow is...' and keep writing for five minutes. Put down everything you can think of about the color yellow. Can you remember a visit to Italy and standing at the edge of a field of yellow sunflowers or do you associate it with lumpy school custard?

Don't censor what you write. At the end of five minutes, underline any bits you particularly like and see how you can develop them further.

Writing Exercise 2

Write a story on the theme of 'fire.' This could centre round an argument over a garden bonfire, someone gazing into the flames of a coal fire and remembering something or someone getting made redundant from their job. (Make a list of possible stories you could write from this trigger).

Keep the list in a notebook so you are never stuck for something to write about if you have a few spare moments.

Writing Exercise 3

Create a story about someone buying a yellow silk dress from a charity shop to wear to a party. What happens to them?

List ten possible outcomes and write up the most interesting ones into a story.

Visualization

You may find it helps to read this onto a Dictaphone or ask a friend to do so for you.

Have pen and paper handy so that you can record your ideas immediately after the visualization.

Sit comfortably in your chair. Relax your shoulders. Close your eyes. Breathe deeply in and out. Let go of any tension. Allow each breath to take you further into your creative space.

Follow the pathway ahead of you that leads towards a small hump-back stone bridge that is bathed in golden sunlight. Feel how the sun has warmed the stone. Notice how you feel relaxed as you cross the bridge and follow the pathway towards the edge of a field of sunflowers.

The sky above you is blue with no clouds.

Focus on one of the sunflowers. Look carefully at the soft brown pattern of seeds in the centre and the silky texture of the yellow petals. Draw energy from both light and color and allow this to feed your creative spark.

Focus on the flower for a few moments before moving on along the pathway.

In a few moments you reach a clearing surrounded by tall trees where you notice a steaming black cauldron. Breathe in the spicy lemon smell rising from it as you focus on the characters in your story. What sort of people are they? Who is the main character? What do they look like? What do they most want from life? What is stopping them from achieving this?

Move closer and look at the surface of the bubbling yellow liquid. Allow both color and smell to energize you and then, when you are ready, make you way back along the pathway, past the sunflowers, over the sunlit bridge and back along the pathway towards your own space so that you are back in the place where you began your journey.

Allow yourself to become aware of your surroundings, noticing taste and smell and the darkness behind your closed eyes. Stretch, yawn, wriggle your fingers and toes. Open your eyes. As soon as you feel able, record your journey in as much detail as possible.

The Work

If your characters are weak or unconvincing, then your readers will very quickly put the book down.

Give your readers a reason to care about the outcome of the story. Build as much life and energy into the characters as you can.

Use 'method acting' techniques to follow your characters through a typical day. What is the first thing they do and hear when they get out of bed in the morning? What sort of bed do they sleep in? For instance, your main character might wake to the sound of her mother lighting the fire downstairs and the smell of bacon frying. The first thing she might do before she gets out of bed is to put her socks on so that she's protected from the icy cold lino on the floor.

What sort of clothes do your characters wear? Are the clothes their choice or someone else's? How do they walk? What do they eat and how do they eat it? For example do they put mayonnaise on everything they eat or do they have a craving for chocolate when they're stressed?

What do they look like? Keep a careful note of hair and eye color and make sure this doesn't change by the end of the book – unless there's a reason for the main character dyeing his/her hair and buying colored contact lenses!

Think carefully about what their childhood was like. Even if the character is 45 when they first set foot on the pages of your story, what happened when they were younger will have shaped the person they are now.

Look for magazine pictures or old photos that remind you of the characters. If the book was made into a film, who would you cast in the various parts?

Character Questionnaire

What is their full name? Do they have a nickname?
When is their birthday? What star sign are they?
Do they have brothers and sisters?
What was their childhood like?
Were they the favorite child? If not, how did that make them feel?
What was their favorite toy/game?
What was their favorite color/food?
Did they enjoy school?
What is their most precious possession? Who gave it to them?
How do they dress?
What work do they do?
What is their attitude to money/timekeeping?
What interests do they have?
Are they a day or night person?
What is their attitude to food/sex?

What was their best subject at school?

Do they have loads of friends or are they a loner?

What does your character most want from life?

What is stopping them from achieving this?

A series of obstacles is needed to prevent your character getting what they want too easily. (This is where the various 'conflicts' come in!)

Don't make your good characters too perfect or your bad ones too evil. Give them all flaws and redeeming features.

Kitchen, Bathroom and Bedroom

Follow your characters through the day. Can they cook or do they rely on take-aways? Is their kitchen immaculate or is it a cheerful muddle of bubbling pots and pans, children's pictures on the fridge and a cat or dog sitting by the fire?

Do they wash up regularly or is the sink full of dirty crockery? Do they have a cleaning lady?

Does your character prefer a bath or a shower? What brand of soap or shower gel do they use?

What is their usual routine in the bathroom? How long does it take them?

Does your heroine wear make-up? Is she careful about removing it before she goes to bed or does the hero get irritated because she regularly gets mascara on his white linen pillowcases?

Do they hang their clothes up when they get undressed or are they left like sloughed skins on the floor? What do they wear in bed? Do they fall asleep quickly or lie awake worrying about something? What do they do if they can't sleep – e.g. count sheep, drink tea or get up and do some work?

Do a random check at different times of the day and think 'how would my character behave in this situation?'

Your characters should have changed in some way by the end of the story. For instance, a woman who is in danger of becoming a doormat at the beginning of the story may get a 'wake up' call and start to take charge of her life. By the end of the story we see her with a new man, a smarter appearance and a new job.

Green

The Heart Chakra

This chakra controls the heart, lungs, breasts, hands and arms. An imbalance can lead to emotional problems.

The day of the week relating to this chakra is Friday.

The musical note is F.

Introduce the color to your workspace by buying green or pink candles or cushions.

Collect the following crystals:

moss agate

aventurine

emerald

jade

Use the following oils or incense sticks:

geranium

hyacinth

lilac

rose

vanilla

Grow a pot of thyme on your windowsill and use the chopped leaves in your cooking and in salads.

Try the following recipe:

Creamy Baked Cabbage and Bacon

1 head of green cabbage
1 tbsp butter
half a cup of sliced onion
2 cloves of garlic
1 tbsp fresh thyme leaves
half a cup of diced bacon
black pepper
quarter of a cup of white wine
one third of a cup of thick cream

Chop the cabbage and boil for 2 – 3 minutes. Drain and set aside.

Turn the oven to 375F

In a large oven-proof skillet melt the butter on a low heat. Add the onion
and bacon. Cook for five minutes.

Chop and crush the garlic. Add to the onion with the fresh thyme and black pepper.

Cook for five more minutes.

Add the cabbage and toss with the other ingredients until the excess liquid has been absorbed.

Add the white wine and simmer until reduced.

Add the cream and put in the oven for 30 minutes

Writing Exercises

Writing Exercise 1

Begin with 'green is...' and keep writing for five minutes. Don't stop, cross out or edit. Include everything you can think of about the color green. Can you remember rolling down a grassy slope when you were a child? Think about the places where you used to play. Are there any details or feelings you could include in your story?

What games did your main character play when they were young?

Writing Exercise 2

How does your main character feel about the smell of cut grass? Does it conjure up memories for him/her of being sent to bed early on summer evenings and hearing the sound of lawnmowers through the open window?

Write for five minutes about your main characters favorite things e.g. the smell of lavender, the taste of dark chocolate, the texture of velvet, black and white films and listening to jazz.

Writing Exercise 3

What was your favorite food when you were a child? Were you ever made to eat something you didn't like? What happened if you didn't?

What do you remember about the kitchen of the house you lived in when you were a child? What did it smell like? What did your mother cook? Did she enjoy doing it?
What was the atmosphere like?

Set the kitchen timer for five minutes and write about this as fully as you can. At the end of the time, underline any bits that may be useful for stories or poems.

Could this form part of the background to one of your characters?

Visualization

You may find it helpful to read this onto a Dictaphone first – or ask a friend with a soothing voice to do so.

Have pen and paper handy so that you can record your ideas immediately.

Sit comfortably in your chair or lie on the floor. Relax your shoulders. Close your eyes. Breathe deeply in and out allowing each breath to take you deeper into your creative relaxation.

When you are ready, follow the path ahead of you towards a small wooden bridge. The sun is warm as you look down at the clear water of a stream as it tumbles over rocks below the bridge.

What can you see as you gaze into the water? What does it sound like as it tumbles over the rocks?

Cross the bridge and follow the narrow pathway that winds gradually uphill towards a small copse of oak trees.

Sit on the bench at the top, sheltered by the canopy of leaves and look down at the green landscape spread below you.

The sun is shining and there is a light breeze ruffling the long grass in the distance making it look like waves on an inland sea.

Breathe gently in and out and absorb the color green as you look towards some trees in the middle of the next field, noticing the patterns their leaves make against the blue sky.

Think about the emotional situations in the story you are writing. Have you developed these enough? Have you remembered to include details of changing seasons and weather? Have you remembered to use the senses – colors, sounds, smells and textures – to give your reader a full picture?

Sit for a few moments watching the movement of grass and leaves. Allow any new ideas about your story to come to you. Remember these as you prepare to make your way back down the winding path, over the wooden bridge, along the pathway and back into your own space.

Allow yourself to feel settled back in your chair. Stretch, yawn, wriggle your fingers and toes. Open your eyes.

As soon as you feel able, record your journey in as much detail as possible.

The Work

Where is the action taking place? Is this clear in each scene or are some events taking place in a vacuum?

Use the thoughts and feelings of the characters to add more

detail. Remember that no two people will see a place in the same way. One character may feel soothed by the scent of lavender as she walks along an overgrown garden path, remembering her grandmother's orderly linen cupboard and comfortable spare bed, whereas another may be reminded of visits to an aunt who was unkind to her.

Think of places you know well and adapt them for use in your stories. The writer Stephen King goes back time and again in his imagination to the places he played as a child and uses them as settings for his novels. The places he remembers disappeared long ago under parking lots and houses, but they still exist in his mind.

The seasons need to change as the story develops. Think about light patterns and how they change through the day and the seasons.

Use the senses when describing a place. For instance, what does a character notice when he/she walks along a street? One character may notice the smell of coffee through the open door of a café whereas another may notice petrol fumes or a woman's perfume as she passes them.

Be specific. Think about brand names and include them as a touch of authenticity. Setting is time, place and historical detail.

Develop the collages, scrapbooks and storyboards you started at the beginning of this process. If using a real place, check any facts and do any necessary research. (Don't let this hold you up with the writing process!)

Many writers draw maps of imaginary settings or create 3D images from Plasticine or Fimo clay.

If you're working on a murder mystery or something where time-scales are particularly important, you would need to work out how long it would take a character to travel from one place to another.

What would a character see on their journey? Would this vary with the time of year – for instance would they see more of another house or garden when a particular tree loses its leaves in the autumn?

The mood and emotions of your characters will influence whether they see a place in a positive or negative way – and whether they are there from choice or because they have to be there.

Visualize settings so that you can see, hear and smell them clearly. If they are real to you, they will be to your reader.

If it is safe to do so, when visiting a setting, it is a good idea to close your eyes and pay attention to any sounds or smells that you may not have noticed with your eyes open. For instance, you may be more aware of traffic sounds or birdsong. You may notice the smell of roses or an overflowing rubbish bin nearby. How would a blind person experience the place? What would they notice?

If possible, take a Dictaphone or sound recorder with you. Whatever you record may be useful for background information.

Take lots of photos or do sketches of places at different times of day. Don't censor your photos! I gained a new character for one of my novels as a result of a photo that went wrong.

Collect menus and paper napkins from cafes.

Remember that your setting can be a factor in helping to sell your book. Look at how well novels set in places like Paris or New York sell.

This is also true of imaginary settings as long as you make the experience real for your readers.

Blue

The Throat Chakra

This chakra controls the mouth, neck, shoulders and the passages going to the ears. An imbalance or blockage can lead to sore throats, swollen glands, mouth ulcers and ear problems.

The day of the week relating to this chakra is Wednesday.

The musical note is G.

Introduce the color to your workspace by buying a sky blue candle.
Collect the following crystals:

blue lace agate

lapis lazuli

sapphire

turquoise

Burn the following incense or fragrant oils:

fennel

lavender

lemongrass

valerian

Grow a pot of parsley on your windowsill or desk and use it to flavor your cooking and in salads.

Try the following recipe:

Parsley Bread

Preparation time: 2 hours
Cooking time: 45 minutes

Three quarters of a cup of warm water
Dried yeast
Half a cup of milk – at room temperature
1 tsp sugar
1 tsp salt
2 tbsp chopped fresh parsley
2 tbsp soft butter
3 cups of bread flour

In a large bowl mix the warm water and yeast.

Add milk, sugar, salt, parsley and butter. Stir well.

Add 2 cups of bread flour and mix well so that you create a dough that follows the spoon around the bowl.

Turn the dough out onto a lightly floured surface. Knead for 10 minutes adding more bread flour as needed until the dough is firm and smooth to the touch. Place in a medium sized greased bowl.

Turn the dough over so the top is lightly greased.

Cover with a cloth and leave to rise in a warm place for an hour.

Punch down the dough. Turn onto a floured surface. Knead for five minutes or until the air bubbles are out of the bread.

Shape into an oval loaf. Put on a greased baking sheet. Cut three diagonal slashes about a quarter of an inch deep across the top.

Cover and leave to rise for 45 minutes until the loaf has doubled in size.

Bake for 45 minutes or until the loaf sounds hollow when tapped. Cool on a rack.

Writing Exercises

Writing Exercise 1

Set the timer and write for five minutes about the color blue. How many different types of blue can you think of – e.g. sky, cobalt, air force, navy, royal and azure? Collect some blue color charts from a DIY store. Pick a color and see if you can create a story from it.

Writing Exercise 2

"Something old, something new, something borrowed and something blue..." Write a story about a wedding.

Set the timer and write for five minutes without stopping. Write down everything you can think of about weddings. Think about dreams and nightmares, your own experience as a bridesmaid or page boy or some aspect of your family history.

Underline any sections that could be useful memories or experiences for your characters.

Writing Exercise 3

Combine the following elements into a story: an unexpected letter, a song, a pair of gloves, a journey and the color blue.

Begin by free-writing about this for five minutes so that you trip up the little voice in your head that says "you can't write about that…"

Visualization

You may find it helpful to record this on a Dictaphone first.

Have pen and paper handy so that you can record your ideas immediately after your visualization.

Sit comfortably in your chair. Relax your shoulders. Close your eyes. Breathe deeply in and out. Allow each out breath to take you deeper into your creative relaxation as you imagine yourself walking along a sunlit path.

The sun is warm on your skin as you walk slowly. Allow yourself to relax more with each step you take.

Keep walking until you reach a blue wooden gate that leads to a flower meadow. Open the gate and go in. Take time to look around you. The birds are singing and the atmosphere is peaceful. The meadow is a living carpet of soft grass and wild flowers – daisies, buttercups, blue speedwell and many others. You can hear the gentle drone of bees in the hedgerows that surround the meadow.

Lie on the grass and breathe in the hay-like smell as you gaze up at the clear blue sky.

Soft white clouds are moving across the sky like a slow-moving film. Focus on the pictures they make. If they were characters in your story, who would they be? Or are the clouds like speech bubbles not yet filled in? What do your characters sound like? Do they sound different from each other? If not, what can you change so that they do?

Focus on the patterns in the sky and ask the clouds to show you any missing parts of your story. Remember these ideas as you slowly get up and prepare to leave the meadow, going out of the blue wooden gate and closing it behind you.

Make your way back along the sunlit path until you reach the place you started from and are sitting comfortably back in your chair.

Stretch, yawn, wriggle your fingers and toes. Open your eyes. As soon as you feel able, record your journey in as much detail as possible.

The Work

When we hear the characters speak, it brings them to life.

The function of dialogue in a story is to:

- show the characters in action
- give more information about the setting
- give more information about the plot
- increase dramatic tension

Begin by getting the bones of the story down on paper. Map out any dramatic exchanges of dialogue. Then go back as many times as you need to in order to get the individual voices right.

Dialogue is a good medium for springing surprises and allows the reader to find out more about the characters and how they behave in a variety of situations.

Make sure that they sound different from each other and their names are not too similar. It can be very confusing if there's a Dave, Don, Dora and Dina in the same story!

Spend some time 'listening' to your characters. What are their particular catch phrases or patterns of speech? Create an information sheet for each character so that you are clear about what the voices are like.

Write a scene in dialogue without the 'he said' 'she said.' It is sometimes stronger to have a line of dialogue and then a line of action to clarify who is speaking – for example: "I don't know how you could be so stupid." Rob scanned the bank statement again, his face white with anger.

Put it away for a week or so and then re-read it. Is it clear who is speaking? If not, what can you do to make the voices different?

Think about facial expression – and the fact that what characters say may not be what they actually mean. A sly look observed in a mirror when a man is expressing his love for a woman he wants to borrow money from might not only betray his true feelings but also put an end to his wicked plans.

Remember that you are not writing a court transcript – story dialogue is like real conversation with the boring bits taken out. Use only what is important to the story. If a line of dialogue doesn't either give information or move the action forward, then get rid of it.

Dialogue should sound natural – not like a question and answer session. Contract words wherever possible e.g. 'he'd' not 'he had', 'couldn't' instead of 'could not', 'would've' instead of 'would have' – unless you are writing an historical novel where some of the voices may sound more formal.

If you are writing something historical, then check out the language that was in common usage in the 'Slang Dictionary' – available in most libraries.
Similarly, if one of your characters has a foreign or regional accent, just give a flavor of this and then get on with the story! It can be distracting to read dialogue that has been too faithfully represented and looks like an army of tadpoles moving across the page.

Read dialogue aloud. It will help you spot any dodgy bits. Highlight with a marker pen any bits that drag or don't sound convincing. Be ruthless and cut anything that doesn't work.

If any sections of narrative seem a bit slow, adding dialogue will speed up the action. If the pace is too frantic, converting short sections to narrative will slow things down.

If you are asked to reduce your word count, check through each scene and see if there is any dialogue that can be cut or abbreviated in order to achieve this. It may be that in some cases a short summary will give the necessary information, leaving more words available to create a dramatic scene later in the story.

Indigo

The Third Eye Chakra

This chakra controls the eyes, ears and brain and is the channel for wisdom – past, present and future. An imbalance or blockage may give blurred vision, headaches/migraine, blocked sinuses, insomnia and nightmares.

The day of the week relating to this chakra is Thursday.

The musical note is A.

Introduce the color to your workspace by buying a deep blue candle or cushion.

Collect the following crystals:

amethyst

azurite

lapis lazuli

sodalite

Use the following fragrant oils or incense sticks:

sage

sandalwood

thyme

Grow a pot of borage on your desk or windowsill and use the leaves in salads. Try the following recipe:

Strawberry and Borage Cocktail

2 or 3 borage leaves
250ml dry vermouth
450ml orange juice
450ml soda water
450ml ginger ale
1 lemon thinly sliced
1 dozen small strawberries
borage flowers

Lightly crush the borage leaves with pestle and mortar.

Place in large punch bowl and add all other ingredients except strawberries and borage flowers.

Chill. Clean and prepare strawberries and float in punch bowl with borage flowers just before serving.

Candied Borage Flowers

For use on top of small cakes or biscuits to go with cocktail

Pick flowers with small stem when they are quite dry. Paint each one with beaten egg white.

Dust lightly with castor sugar and set to dry in waxed paper in a warm place like an airing cupboard.

Writing Exercises

Writing Exercise 1

Create the beginning of a story set in a bluebell wood. Use as much sensory detail to create a full picture for your reader. For instance, bring in the scent of the bluebells combined with wild garlic and damp earth, the sound of a twig breaking under someone's boot, the mewing of a buzzard.

Begin by free-writing for five minutes. Include everything you can think of that could possible happen in that wood – for example, getting lost, fragments of fairytales, dreams and nightmares about someone chasing you.

Writing Exercise 2

What images does the word 'indigo' conjure up? It always makes me think of old fashioned sailing ships and pirates on the high seas. Let your imagination run riot. Create a different sort of story to what you would normally do. For instance, if you prefer to write historical stories, try fantasy or something for children.

If you're experimenting with a new genre, you may find it helps to create a new persona for yourself!

Writing Exercise 3

Imagine you are in a place you haven't been to before. You go exploring and find a small box. Take time to examine the box carefully before opening it. Inside you find a silver pendant with a lapis lazuli stone in it. You hear someone approaching and put the pendant in your pocket.

What happens next?

Begin by free-writing for five minutes. Allow your imagination to run riot. Then underline any sections that interest you and see if you can create a poem, piece of flash fiction or the beginning of a short story.

Visualization

You may find it helpful to record this on a Dictaphone first – or ask a friend to do so for you.

Have pen and paper handy for immediately after the visualization so that you can record your ideas.

Sit comfortably in your chair. If possible, take off your shoes. Relax your shoulders. Close your eyes. Breathe deeply in and out. Allow each out breath to take you deeper into your creative space as you imagine you are walking along a narrow path edged with tall grass that leads to a shiny black wrought iron gate.

The gate opens easily and you find yourself in a bluebell wood. Keep walking along the pathway and then stop and look around you. Notice how you are surrounded by an indigo blue carpet that stretches amongst the pale trunks of silver birches as far as the eye can see.

Notice the dappled light filtering through the trees and making leaf patterns on the path ahead of you.

Listen to the birdsong that surrounds you. Notice the hyacinth-like scent of the flowers and the waxy texture of the petals and the way the intense carpet of blue looks like the waters of a lake.

Allow the color to relax you as you think of the parts of your story where more sensory detail is needed.

Take a few moments to absorb colors, sounds, smells and textures. Notice other smells, sounds and textures you hadn't noticed before – damp earth and wild garlic, the harsh cry of a jay, the delicate wings of a white butterfly.

When you are ready, turn around and walk slowly back to the black wrought iron gate. Open the gate and go through it, closing it behind you, knowing that you can return here whenever you wish to.

Make your way back along the narrow path edged with tall grass until you arrive back in your own space and are sitting comfortably in your chair.

Sit for a few moments before allowing yourself to slowly wake up. Stretch, yawn, wriggle your fingers and toes. Open your eyes. As soon as you feel able, record your journey in as much detail as possible.

The Work

Have you used the senses as much as possible in your story?

What are the predominant colors of the setting you are writing about? If you were an artist, what colors would you need on your palette to give an impression of the place where the story is set? For instance, a Cornish cliff-top in July might be a riot of yellow gorse and pink thrift whereas a river estuary in January would be milk chocolate and ice blue. Think of interesting ways to describe colors. Look at the decorating leaflets in DIY shops. Use some of the descriptions in your story for added interest.

What can you hear? If your story is set on a beach, think about the cry of seagulls, the excited shrieks of children running in and out of the waves, the yapping of dogs and the sound of a busker strumming an out-of-tune guitar.

What are your characters eating? Food helps to bring a story to life. Think about the smell of vinegar on fish and chips and the texture of crumbly chocolate cake. How do your characters react to food? How would your main character eat a hotdog – or wouldn't they? Imagine each of your characters eating a chocolate éclair. What do they do? For instance would one of them pick it up and lick off the cream first whereas another person ate theirs with a fork, making sure they stayed neat and tidy. (This gives added opportunity for conflict between characters).

Look for new ways to describe settings and the behavior of your characters. This is where writing poetry is useful! In your notebook, jot down 'glimpses' using all the senses. For instance:

blue and gold flames
reflected in a copper warming pan
on the buttermilk café wall

eyes blue as a Mediterranean sea
under a straight black fringe

plump raspberries bursting from
a cream meringue

a pink tongue slowly licking chocolate
from long fingers

the smell of freshly ground coffee

and steamy windows

I snuggle against red velvet cushions and
gaze through the window at
pavements glittering with frost

Use these to create a series of poems about characters and settings.

You could publish these as a separate collection or send them to magazines and competitions.

Take your notebook wherever you go and use it to record any experiences you have – good and bad. For instance, how do you feel when you go to the dentist? What does it feel like when you're in the chair? What can you see, hear and smell?
What is it like when you take your car to the garage for a new tire? What do you notice? How do the people who work in the garage treat you? What are their voices like? Is there a new 'language' here that you don't understand?

Next time you go to the supermarket, see how many story ideas or possible titles you can find from the names of various shower gels or beauty products. Look at the fruits and vegetables on display and see where they have come from. Could you write a story set in one of those places?

Sit in a café and observe the people around you. Look at the color and texture of their clothes. Listen to their voices. If they were a musical instrument, what would they be? If they were a variety of cake or chocolate, what would they be?

Remember to go through your notebook regularly to extract any useful information.

Violet

The Crown Chakra

This chakra controls the brain and psyche. Its element is spirit or ether. An imbalance or blockage may lead to headaches, migraine, poor immune system, forgetfulness and minor accidents.

The day of the week relating to this chakra is Sunday.

The musical note is B.

Introduce the color to your workspace by buying a violet colored candle or cushion.

Collect the following crystals:

white and purple banded amethyst

diamond

pearl

crystal quartz

Use the following fragrant oils or incense sticks:

frankincense

lavender

rosemary

Grow rosemary or marigolds on your windowsill.

Try the following recipe:

Lavender Bread Pudding

1 cup thick cream
2 tsp fresh lavender buds
8 slices white bread – cut and trimmed
Quarter of a cup of butter – room temperature
Quarter of a cup of apricot jam or marmalade
Quarter of a cup of raisins
2 eggs
Half a cup of sugar
Half a cup of milk
2 tsp vanilla
Quarter of a cup of icing sugar
Half a teaspoon of dried crushed lavender buds

Heat the cream in a small saucepan until bubbles form round the edge. Remove from the heat. Add lavender buds and leave to cool.

Grease an 8 x 12 baking dish and preheat the oven to 350F.

Butter bread slices and spread with jam. Arrange four slices in the dish with butter and jam side up. Sprinkle raisins over and top with bread and jam slices – face down.

In a medium bowl beat the eggs and sugar until light and creamy. Whisk in milk and vanilla. Strain cooled cream into the mixture and whisk to combine. Pour over bread and allow to stand for 15 minutes.

Bake for 30 minutes.

Combine crushed lavender and icing sugar in a small bowl. Dust over pudding when it comes out of oven. Serve warm.

Writing Exercises

Writing Exercise 1

Write for five minutes about the color purple. Think about every association it has for you – or for anyone you know! For instance, did your grandmother wear a mauve hat on Sundays or did your favorite doll wear a purple dress? Which day of the week do you associate with purple?

Then begin a story with "My favorite color was always purple until the day when … Let me tell you what happened."

Writing Exercise 2

Write a story set in a bakery where the owner's unusual ideas for cake recipes lead her into trouble.

You may find it helps to begin this exercise by creating a mind-map or spider diagram to generate ideas.

Writing Exercise 3

Begin by writing down as many sensory associations as you can think of to the color purple – e.g. the velvet cushions in your grandmother's sitting room, the Parma Violet sweets you once bought from an old-fashioned sweet shop and the painted violets on your best friend's coffee mug.

Write a story about a ghost who smells of Devon Violets perfume. Who was she and where does she make her appearance? How is the situation resolved?

Visualization

You may find it helpful to record this onto a Dictaphone – or ask a friend to do so.

Have pen and paper beside you so that you can record your ideas immediately after the visualization.

Sit comfortably in your chair. If possible, take off your shoes. Relax your shoulders. Close your eyes. Breathe deeply in and out. Imagine each out breath taking you deeper into your creative space as you follow a sunlit pathway towards a wooden bridge painted shiny poppy red.

Cross the bridge and follow the wide circular path on the other side in a clockwise direction. The path is edged with lavender on each side and you absorb the scent as you walk.

Bees drone lazily amongst the flowers, the sun is warm and the fragrance of lavender relaxes you more with every step.

Focus on any loose ends of your story and anything you have not yet finished. See solutions to these problems and visualize your completed novel, seeing your name on the cover, as you keep walking round the wide circle and back towards the red wooden bridge.

Thank the circle before you leave. Cross the bridge and make your way along the narrow path and back into your own space.

Sit for a few moments, eyes closed, absorbing the images you have experienced. Then stretch, yawn, wriggle your fingers and toes. Open your eyes. As soon as you feel able, record your journey in as much detail as possible.

The Work

When you've completed your first draft

Reward yourself!

You've already achieved far more than a great many people.

Put your work away for a few weeks and do something else – work in the garden, bake cakes, refill your creative well.

When you go back to your novel, don't be disappointed if it doesn't match the wonderful picture in your head. Keep going. It will get there. Most novels go through several drafts and re-writes which enable ideas and characters to develop and grow. Don't be afraid to let your ideas change.

If you've been using a working title up till now, spend some time thinking of an attention-grabbing title. Spend time browsing in bookshops and libraries, noticing the ones that have the most impact on you.

Presentation

Most publishers or agents prefer to see a synopsis and the first three chapters, so it is important to get these as good as you possibly can before you send your work out. (Do make sure the book is finished - or you will create a lot of stress for yourself if they ask to see the rest of it!)

Some publishers require a smaller number of words, but they will ask you to complete a Publisher Enquiry Form which will tell them if you're the sort of writer they want on their list. The questions on this will include things about your previous writing experience and whether or not you are prepared to help promote the book. (The answer to this should, of course, be YES!)

Check the individual submission guidelines and send them exactly what they are asking for in the format they require.

As a rough guide these will include things like:

- Use wide margins

- 12 font Times New Roman or Arial.

- Don't staple or bind pages – an elastic band will do

- Type on one side of the paper only

- Unless told otherwise, indent the first line of each paragraph and the first line of each new piece of dialogue

- Number pages

It's a good idea to put your name and the title of your book in the footer so that if the manuscript falls off an editor's desk it can be re-assembled quickly.

Do not send by email unless they specify that you can. If posting, send return postage if you would like your manuscript back. Some writers give instructions to shred the manuscript if it is not required and notify the decision by email.

Synopsis

Many writers worry more about the synopsis than they do about writing the rest of the book! The synopsis should give a flavor of your novel and should be presented single spaced. Write in the present tense and follow the guidelines of the individual agent or publisher as to whether they want a shorter American style synopsis (usually only one page) or something a bit longer.

Include the following elements:

- Title
- Approximate word count of finished novel
- Your name and contact details
- Genre (where the book will fit on the shelves)
- Theme
- Setting
- Who the main characters are
- Brief outline of main plot
- Mention any subplots
- Key scenes/main conflict situations
- Brief fragments of dialogue
- Final outcome

Remember this is the selling document for the book. Keep paragraphs short so that it looks easy to read. (Imagine how an editor may feel at the end of a long day!) Focus on the action of the story. Be as descriptive as possible. Include lots of color and sensory detail and a 'narrative hook' that will make the reader want to reach for the first chapter.

Covering Letter

Your covering letter should be brief and business-like. Mention any previous publication successes and any special features with this book that may help in the marketing process.

For instance, if the main action of the novel happens in a garden and you are a member of a gardening club with 500 members, this may well guarantee some sales for the publisher and make him more interested in your work.

An interesting or well-described location can also be a factor in increased sales of a book. I remember 'Weekend in Paris' by Robyn Sisman selling well at the Eurostar Terminal in London a few years ago.

DON'T include a list of names of friends and relatives who have read your novel and say it's the best thing they've ever read. This is unlikely to impress a publisher or agent.

Enclose a self addressed postcard so that they can confirm receipt. Attach a receipt when emailing.

When you've posted or emailed your novel, have a break for a few days before you start planning your next project. Don't pester the publisher or agent. It can take at least three to four months for them to come to a decision.

Rejection

If your work isn't accepted this time, don't be too downhearted. Even famous writers get work rejected. It is part of the publication process.

Don't take it personally! Allow yourself a few hours to grieve, console yourself with chocolate, a glass of wine or a restorative walk in the countryside and then get on with following your dream.

Look carefully at any comments made and see if you feel they are justified. Sometimes you are just not on the same wave-length as that person. Work that is rejected by one publisher or agent may be snapped up by another.

Don't spend time feeling sorry for yourself or emailing your friends to say how upset you feel. Send the story out again within 48 hours and start planning your launch party!

If more than three publishers make the same comment, then it might be a good idea to look at your work again or think about having a professional critique. Again, shop around for a reasonable price and someone whose opinion you trust.

Keep a note of any positive comments you receive about your work and look at them when you are feeling despondent. Make a collage of them and put it on the wall of your workspace.

Do something creative with the rejection slips. One writer I met had created a papier maché model.

Have as many pieces of work as possible in circulation – short pieces as well as novels. You will achieve small successes along the way and the more work you have out there, the less you will worry about rejection and start to see it as part of your apprenticeship as a writer.

Staying Motivated

Keep visualizing your ideal life. Remember the four rules of visualization:

1. Be clear about what you want to achieve and what you will gain as a result.

2. If you want to write a novel, see the finished result clearly in your mind and focus on it regularly. Visualize your name on the cover, run your fingers over the letters.

3. Take active steps towards your goal – i.e. WRITE!

4. Create images that bring your finished novel to life – e.g. collages. Write about your ideal life and how others will benefit from this.

Use the senses as much as you can. What will you hear, see, smell, feel and taste when your book is published?

By creating specific images and positive energy, you will draw success towards you.

For instance, when I was focusing on my first novel 'Fable's Fortune', I imagined:

- the color purple
- the sound of gypsy violins
- the texture of velvet
- the smell of bread baking
- the taste of violet cream chocolates

Have something in your workspace that reminds you of at least one of these. I had a piece of amethyst and a red velvet cushion that were constant reminders to think of color and textures. Before each writing session, I lit a candle scented with lily of the valley that gave a flavor of the garden where some of the action took place.

Keep a special notebook and write something about your ideal life every day. Even two or three lines, written regularly will add strength to your dream. Focus on building a clear picture by using the senses. Also think about how you and those you love might benefit from your success.

Take time to refill the creative well on a regular basis. Spend time walking in the countryside, visit a gallery or a new café or go for an Indian Head Massage. Eat plenty of fruit and vegetables and drink lots of water. Take regular breaks from your desk to do some stretches and focus your eyes on something outside the window.

Sometimes we all need a break! If your ideas aren't flowing, try one or two of the following ideas:

If your ideas aren't flowing

Try some of the following ideas if you hit a bad patch when you feel 'stuck.'

- If your book was turned into a film, what would the sound-track be like? Create a sound-track and dance to it. Move your body in clockwise spirals. You may find that your ideas begin to flow.

- Listen to the sort of music your characters would like. Does this give you further ideas about them or a new twist to the plot?

- Soak in a scented bath with a glass of wine.

- Go shopping and buy something your main character would like. If it's not too big, keep it on your desk for inspiration.

- Sit in a café you've not visited before and do some people-watching. You may overhear something that sparks a fresh idea.

- Work in the garden. Sow some seeds. Pull up weeds.

- Ask 'what if' questions about situations and characters. Use the Conflict Circle and see if that generates some new ideas.

- Add more pictures to your scrapbook or storyboard. Do some research in the Library or on Google.

- Write a letter or email from one character to another.

- List your main character's interests and find out more about one of them. For instance, if your character dabbles in witchcraft, visit a local herb garden and spend some time looking at the plants and noticing the texture and smell of the leaves and flowers.

Create your writing C.V.

If you're serious about getting published in the future, then start building your writing persona now! Don't wait until your book is about to be published. Create a space for you and your book to walk into and be recognized.

Work on shorter pieces of writing and get into the habit of sending them off regularly. Create deadlines for yourself and stick to them. If this was your official day job you'd do it, wouldn't you?

Offer to write a regular column for your local paper – whether there is payment involved or not. It will get your name recognized and will also give your good practice in submitting work and keeping to deadlines.

Generate as many new ideas from a single inspiration as you can. Many of my poems originate from a piece of overhead conversation in a café or on a train and may then be developed into:

- a shorter or longer poem than the original
- a piece of flash fiction (a complete story up to 500 words in length)
- a monologue
- a longer story
- a scene from a novel or play
- song lyrics

Don't be afraid to experiment. In the past I've been very successful when I haven't really known what I was doing. Don't wait for permission – go for it!

Develop your 'writer's voice.' The more you write, the sooner this will happen.

Aim to have a minimum of ten pieces of work in circulation at a time. Keep good records of where you have sent your work – and also of any money received.

One of the best pieces of advice I ever had was to complete my second novel before I sent the first one out. Promoting a book takes time and energy. You don't want to be under pressure to produce new writing at the same time.

Build Your Writers' Network

There has never been a better time to network with other writers all over the world. The ones I have 'met' continue to provide me with the most amazing support and encouragement.

A publisher or agent is likely to ask the following questions:

- Do you have a website?
- Do you have a Blog?
- Are you active on Facebook and Twitter?

The answer to all three questions should be YES!

Your website only needs to be simple, but it will give you a presence that can be developed as your writing gains momentum. Aim for something that looks both interesting and professional. Check that spelling and layout are correct.

If you have a Blog with membership, you could offer a monthly competition which would add interest and generate visitors.

Go to Conferences, festivals, book signings and talks by writers. Most of them will give helpful advice and encouragement to new writers.

Finally…

Remember that even the most famous novelists have had work rejected many times.

Don't give up at the first obstacle. Keep going.

Write the best story possible. Build lots of life and color into it. Use the senses. Engage the emotions of the reader so that they want to carry on with the story.

Be persistent.

If you feel you've done a good piece of work have faith in it. Keep going until a publisher or agent says yes.

Enjoy your journey towards publication.

Help others on the same pathway.

Magazines For Writers

Writers' News/Writing Magazine
Warners Group Publications plc
31-32 Park Row
Leeds LS1 5JD
Tel: 0113 200 2929
www.writingmagazine.co.uk

Writers' Forum
Select Publishers Services Ltd
P O Box 6337
Bournemouth
BH1 9EH
Tel: 01202 568848

Mslexia
P O Box 656
Newcastle-upon-Tyne
NE99 1PZ
Tel: 0191 233 3860
www.mslexia.co.uk

The New Writer
P O Box 60
Cranbrook
Kent TN17 2ZR

Facts & Fiction
42 Mill Street
Belper
Derbyshire
DE56 1DT
www.factsandfiction.co.uk

Books For Writers

'Becoming a Writer'
by Dorothea Brande
pub. Penguin Putnam ISBN 0-87477-164-1

'The Artist's Way'
by Julia Cameron
pub. Pan ISBN 0-330-34358-0

'The Vein of Gold'
by Julia Cameron
pub. Pan ISBN: 0-330-35285-7

'Write it down – make it happen'
by Henriette Anne Klauser
pub. Simon & Schuster ISBN 0-743-20938-9

'Indestructible Self Belief'
by Fiona Harrold
pub. Piatkus ISBN 0-7499-2495-0

'Writing down the bones'
by Natalie Goldberg
pub. Shambhala ISBN 1-57062-424-0

'A Writer's Space'
by Eric Maisel
pub. Adams Media ISBN: 978-59869-460-4

'The Weekend Novelist'
by Robert Ray and Brett Norris
pub. A & C Black ISBN: 0-7136-7143-2

'On Writing'
by Stephen King
pub. New English Library ISBN: 0-340-82048-2

'The Writer's Toolkit' booklets
by Sue Johnson
pub. Greenwood Press
www.writers-toolkit.co.uk

Websites For Writers

Arvon Foundation
60 Farringdon Road
London EC1R 3GA
www.arvonfoundation.org

National Association of Writers' Groups
P O Box 9891
Market Harborough
LE16 0FU
email: secretary@nawg.co.uk

Romantic Novelists Association
www.romanticnovelistsassociation.org

Society of Authors
84 Drayton Gardens
London SW10 9SB
Tel: 0207 373 6642

Nielsen Book Data UK
www.isbn.nielsenbook.co.uk

BBC Writers Room
1st Floor Grafton House
379 – 381 Euston Road
London NW1 3AU
email: writersroom@bbc.co.uk

Writers Guild of Great Britain
40 Rosebery Avenue
London EC1R 4RX
email: writersguild@aptsolutions.co.uk

**COMPASS
BOOKS**

Compass Books focuses on practical and informative 'how-to' books for writers. Written by experienced authors who also have extensive experience of tutoring at the most popular creative writing workshops, the books offer an insight into the more specialised niches of the publishing game.

The Writer's Toolkit
www.writers-toolkit.co.uk